SLEEP TIGHT!

AN ACTIVITY BOOK TO HELP YOUNG PEOPLE SLEEP SOUNDLY EVERY NIGHT

Kane Miller
A DIVISION OF EDC PUBLISHING

First American Edition 2021
Kane Miller, A Division of EDC Publishing

© 2021 Studio Press

Written by Dr. Sharie Coombes
Illustrated by Katie Abey
Designed by Rob Ward
Edited by Frankie Jones

First published in the UK in 2021 by Studio Press, an imprint of Bonnier Books UK

For information contact:
Kane Miller, A Division of EDC Publishing
5402 S. 122nd E. Ave, Tulsa, OK 74146

www.kanemiller.com
www.usbornebooksandmore.com

Library of Congress Control Number: 2020949043

FSC
www.fsc.org

MIX
Paper from
responsible sources
FSC® C104723

Printed in China
1 3 5 7 9 10 8 6 4 2

ISBN: 978-1-68464-276-2

SLEEP TiGHT!

THIS BOOK BELONGS TO

— — — — — — — — — —

WELCOME TO SLEEP TIGHT!

Author
DR. SHARIE COOMBES
Child and Family Psychotherapist

Everyone finds it hard to drop off to sleep, or to stay asleep, from time to time, and this fun activity book is a great way to get you ready for happier bedtimes and better sleep. You'll find out how to deal with whatever is standing in your way so that you can get the sleep you need to enjoy life to the fullest. It's time to SLEEP TIGHT!

Doing these activities will help you to understand and express what makes bedtimes tricky and stops you from sleeping soundly. You'll learn how to prepare for a great bedtime, how to rest and relax more during the day, how to combat your concerns, feel more in control and confident about sleeping, and discover ways to tell adults about your worries (if you want to). You could use this book in a quiet, comfortable place at any time during the day, and it's great to use it in bed as well. You might do a page a day or complete lots of pages at one time. You can start anywhere in the book and come back to a page many times. There are no rules!

Sometimes worries feel enormous, and you might believe nothing will help, but there is always a solution to every problem. Nothing is so big that it can't be sorted out or talked about, even if it feels that way. You could show some of these activities to important people in your life to help you explain how you are feeling and to get some help. You can talk to an adult you trust at school, or ask an adult at home to take you to the doctor for support.

Lots of children need extra help every now and then, and here are two organizations you can turn to if you don't want to talk to people you know. They have helped thousands of children with every kind of problem and will know how to help you. They won't be shocked by what you tell them, however bad it feels to you.

CHILDHELP

Childhelp is dedicated to looking after children.

Their free, confidential help line puts you in touch with a counselor any time, day or night.

Tel: 1-800-422-4453   www.childhelp.org

YOUR LIFE YOUR VOICE

Help, tips, and tools offering great advice about a wide range of issues for children and young people 24 hours a day. Free mood tracker app and counseling by helpline, text, and email.

Tel: 1-800-448-3000

Text: VOICE to 20121

Email: Click the email button on the website: www.yourlifeyourvoice.org

BUDDY BEAR AND BOB

MEET
BUDDY
BEAR!

Once upon a time in a faraway cave, Buddy Bear found it very difficult to get to sleep. He often lay in bed for hours, feeling more and more upset. When he had bad dreams, or just woke up, he couldn't get back to sleep because he was afraid of the dark. Buddy Bear didn't understand what was happening and couldn't explain his feelings to any of the other bears. He began to dread bedtime and often made a huge fuss, which only made the problem feel a hundred times worse. He was stuck in the habit of not being able to sleep, so he was grumpy and couldn't concentrate during the day.

WHAT CHANGED?

Buddy Bear told an adult bear in his den about the problems he was having. He found out all about Bob, and TA-DA, now HE is the sleep expert YOU need!

Bob is ancient and lives in the limbic part of the brain.

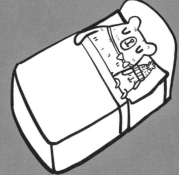

All mammals have a Bob in their brains. Bob's a busy guard dog who thinks EVERYTHING is dangerous and keeps yapping all night — if you let him.

If Bob doesn't rest and relax during the daytime, he gets stressed and finds it even harder to get to sleep at night. Buddy Bear gives his Bob cuddles and comfort at bedtime.

Now, every night is a great-sleep night! Buddy Bear enjoys bedtimes again and sleeps like... yes, you've guessed it, like a bear!

HAPPY BOB, HAPPY YOU!

Ready to give Bob some of what he needs? Great — you're in the right place!
Turn the page to find out more...

BOB AND BEDTIMES

BOB NEEDS...

- ☑ 10-11 hours of sleep
- ☑ Rest and relaxation
- ☑ Bedtime routine
- ☑ Melatonin
- ☑ Comfort
- ☒ Screens
- ☑ You've got this!

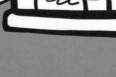

You need 10-11 hours of sleep a night so your muscles can recover, your brain can organize new information, and your organs can catch up on some cleaning.

Creating a bedtime routine trains your mind and body to wind down and prepare for a great night's sleep. This is the time to get all those things that are on your mind out of the way and master keeping Bob happy.

You'll find loads of techniques in this book to help you feel safer, braver, and happier. If you wake from a bad dream and can't get back to sleep, doing one or two SLEEP TIGHT! activities will help.

Your brain makes a chemical called melatonin which eventually sends you off to sleep. Light from screens stops your brain from sending the melatonin, so screens should be switched off around two hours before bed.

Get comfortable – make sure you're not too hot or too cold, you've been to the bathroom, and had a drink if you need one.

If you have ADHD, autism, or anxiety, it can be even harder to get to sleep, but you can do it with Buddy Bear's help.

Look out for Buddy Bear – you'll see him on activities that are good for getting a great night's sleep! If you see Bob, you know the activity is perfect for training him, too. Your great night's sleep is just pages away. Let's SLEEP TIGHT!

SLEEP TIGHT!

How you prepare yourself for bedtime affects how quickly you'll fall asleep and how well you'll sleep through the night. As you explore this book and discover which activities you enjoy, make you feel sleepy, and are the most relaxing, come back to this page and record the activity names on Buddy Bear's duvet.

Whenever you need help to drop off to sleep or you're not feeling sleepy enough, you can come back to Buddy Bear's duvet for a reminder and pick the best activities for you.

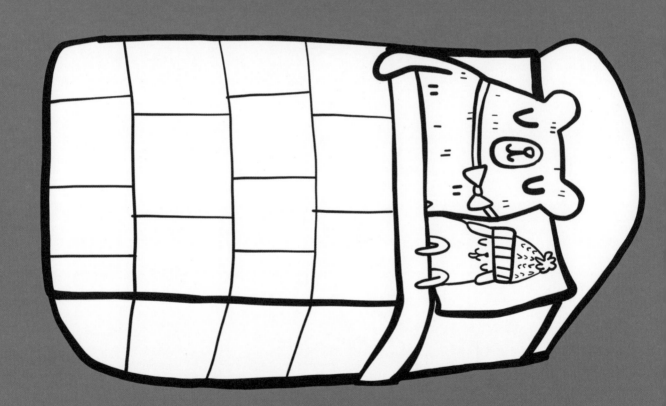

AT THE BACK OF THE BOOK, YOU'LL UNCOVER A WAY TO DESIGN YOUR IDEAL BEDTIME ROUTINE, SO TRYING OUT THE ACTIVITIES IN THIS BOOK AND COMPLETING THIS PAGE WILL BE VERY HELPFUL TO YOU.

HI-BEAR-NATION!

All bears love a great sleep, but it's not always easy for them to drop off and start snoring!

Buddy Bear is looking for friends from around the world to say "Hi!" to, so help him get to know the teddy bear or cuddly toy that helps YOU get to sleep at night.

Draw your own teddy bear or cuddly toy in the picture frame and fill the hearts with descriptions of all the things you love about it. You might write about how it feels to hold, how it smells, how it makes you feel, and how long you've had it, but it's completely up to you. If you've got lots of bedtime friends, pick one you think Buddy Bear would like to chat with.

Don't forget to add your friend's name so that Buddy Bear can say "Hi!"

BEAR NECESSITIES

We all have things we need in order to feel happy and relaxed, and to SLEEP TIGHT!

It can be hard to sleep well if you're unhappy or feel worried. It's important to have moments in the day when you rest and relax. These moments help to keep you healthy and stop you from becoming overtired or stressed.

Write on the bears what you can do, or what you already do, to help you with these necessities. Use some of the examples, and ask an adult to help you if you have trouble thinking of ideas.

Some ideas might work for more than one of your bears – just add them to all the bears they apply to.

EXERCISE

WARM BED

CUDDLES

SURPRISES

READING

GOING FOR A WALK

WATER

RELAXING

ENCOURAGEMENT

LISTENING TO A STORY

HEALTHY FOOD

FRIENDS

FEEL YOU CAN ACHIEVE GOALS

UNBEARABLE TO BEARABLE

If you find it hard to settle or get to sleep, it's possible that you're anxious, stressed, or angry. Do you notice any of these unpleasant feelings? These are caused by an unhappy Bob who is feeling unsafe.

Check any that you notice right now:

☐ FEELING DIZZY, FAINT OR LIGHT-HEADED

☐ FEELING SEPARATE FROM EVERYONE ELSE

☐ FAST BREATHING

☐ HARD TO SWALLOW

☐ TIGHT CHEST

☐ HOT OR COLD FACE AND/OR HANDS

☐ NUMB OR TINGLY FEET

☐ HOT OR COLD WAVES

☐ RACING OR FLUTTERY HEART

☐ FEELING SICK

☐ NUMB OR TINGLY HANDS

☐ FEARFUL OF THE DARK

☐ SWEATY PALMS

☐ TREMBLING OR SHAKING

☐ NOT WANTING TO BE LEFT ALONE

☐ UPSET STOMACH OR BUTTERFLIES

It's a good idea to let your adult know if any of these feelings are getting in your way and to talk through them. Come back to this page any time you need to, so that you can explain what's happening for you. You can look through the book for all the helpful activities featuring Buddy Bear and Bob. They'll give you ideas, show you how to manage these difficult feelings, and support you, so you can get back to feeling relaxed and ready to SLEEP TIGHT!

NIGHT BREATHING

This breathing works during the daytime too, to help you feel relaxed, safe, and calm whenever you need it.

When you breathe out for longer than you breathe in, it calms Bob down and helps him to feel safe. This means you start to relax and feel sleepy enough for a good night ahead.

Here's how to practice breathing at bedtime, both before you get into bed and once you've hopped in:

Start by noticing your breathing for a few minutes. Imagine you are breathing sleepiness in and breathing energy out.

Now you're ready to start 3:5 breathing.

Breathe in for a count of 3, and then slowly out for a count of 5. When you breathe in, see if you can make the sleepiness go all the way into your tummy. Put your hand on your tummy and watch it rise.

When you breathe out, gently push the air out from your tummy, and watch your hand go back down as you let go of the energy. Keep this going for a few minutes until you start to feel sleepier. Once you're in bed, you can keep this going for as long as you like, and imagine you are floating in the starry sky, watching the world from up high as everyone drops off to sleep, one by one.

LOVE
LOCK

Fill this heart with all the people and things you have in your life that help you to feel that you are loved and that you belong.

When you've written or drawn your ideas in the heart, color the lock to close it and lock in all the feelings forever.

Every time you think of something else that can go in your LOVE LOCK, just come back and add it.

Remember, whenever you feel worried or scared, these things are still there inside your LOVE LOCK.

IT'S A RAP!

Buddy Bear loves a good song. Singing at bedtime makes Bob relax so that Buddy Bear – and you – SLEEP TIGHT! Do you know any lullabies?

A lullaby is a short, simple song with a gentle tune to help you relax and feel safe.

Write the words to your favorite lullaby in the moon, or try writing your own song to help Buddy Bear sleep. Make it a rap lullaby if you prefer!

Use the tune to a song you already know, or make one up. If you're stuck for ideas, you could make it about brushing your teeth, finding the right leg hole in your pajamas, being tucked in, or anything else you like.

The next time you feel like a song at bedtime, you know what to do!

THE SAFEST PLACE

Relaxation is a very important part of keeping your body, brain, and mind healthy. If you're someone who loves to be busy, or your mind is always thinking, you may need some practice to be able to relax. If you've been very anxious or stressed, it can sometimes feel a bit strange when you first start relaxing, but keep trying – you'll be glad you did! Everybody's body needs, and deserves, a chance to relax!

It can be really helpful if an adult does this activity with you, so you can follow the instructions as they read them aloud.

NOTE FOR ADULT
Read these instructions slowly, and allow plenty of imagination time between each one. You don't need to ask your child to tell you about their cloud and safe place unless they want to talk about it.

Lie down in your bed, close your eyes, and start 3:5 breathing. Or, if you are doing this by yourself, you can just sit quietly somewhere. Hold your teddy bear or cuddly toy if you like.

Breathe in for 3, slowly and deeply into your tummy, and breathe out for 5, just as slowly.

 Picture yourself climbing onto the softest, squishiest cloud – it's waiting for you next to your bed. It's a very safe cloud that will protect you and keep you warm. Your cloud will only ever do what you want it to do.

Feel the cloud underneath you – is it like a marshmallow? Maybe it's more like a bouncy castle? Or something else...

 Feel the warmth around you, and let your cloud float up high into the sky.

 Take yourself to a place that is the safest place you can imagine. It might be somewhere you've been before, or somewhere you make up.

 Look all around you and notice the colors, shapes, scenery, and people who are there.

 Notice how peaceful, calm, and safe this place feels.

 Enjoy the feeling of safety here. Let it fill you up with a beautiful warm light inside your arms and legs, then your body and brain.

 Stay here for as long as you want, and float on your cloud until you choose to come back, in your own time.

 You can choose a different safe place every time you do this activity if you want to.

 Write about or draw a picture of your safe place, before or after you do this activity. You don't have to do it on the same day.

STORY STICKS

Stories are great at any time of the day and can help to relax you. There's possibly nothing quite as lovely as a story at bedtime to help you SLEEP TIGHT! Sometimes it's even better if you make up your own story with someone else.

Use these story sticks to create an original story every time you try it. You can make up all kinds of stories, including funny and silly ones.

It's a good idea to have different categories for your story sticks, such as:

PLACES AND SETTINGS, FEELINGS, CHARACTERS, DESCRIPTIONS, EVENTS, BEGINNINGS, ENDINGS, PROBLEMS AND CONFLICTS, AND ANY OTHERS YOU CAN THINK OF.

You could even color code the sticks depending on their category.

YOU WILL NEED:

• Some clean craft sticks, or cut out and use these paper ones – you can also glue these onto the craft sticks if you like.

• An envelope or container to keep them in.

• Pens

• Your imagination

• A bedtime!

If you put clear sticky tape over the sticks, you will protect them, and they will last longer. You could also put sticky tape over blank sticks and then use dry-erase pens to keep changing them.

HOW TO USE YOUR STORY STICKS

Start a story using just your imagination, or grab a few story sticks to get you started. You can use as many or as few story sticks as you like.

Use the sticks when you're stuck on what might happen next, and then carry on the story using your imagination again!

ONCE UPON A TIME

THEY LIVED HAPPILY EVER AFTER

SHE WAS A HERO

HE FELT SAD

IN A DEEP, DARK WOOD

ON A HOT, SUNNY DAY

AN ELEPHANT WITH SIX LEGS WEARING A TIGER ONESIE

THEY ALL WENT HOME AND FELL ASLEEP

THE TREE FELL DOWN

ADD YOUR OWN IDEAS TO THESE BLANK STORY STICKS.

TO THE STARS AND BACK

Any time someone does something kind for you, pays you a compliment, or shows you how much they care about you, write it in the star's tail. Remember to look at it from time to time to remind yourself that you are loved to the stars and back!

OVERNIGHT MIRACLE

If a miracle could happen overnight, what one thing would you change for the better?

Color in the rainbow, and as you do, imagine this change really has happened.

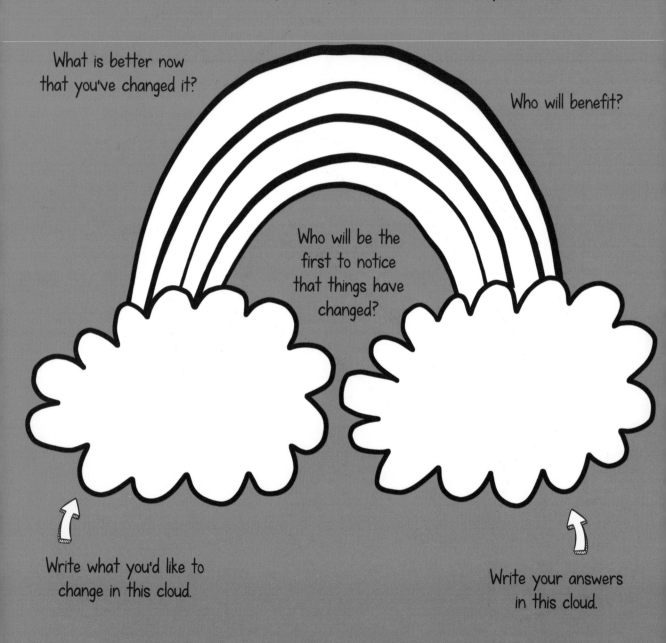

What is better now that you've changed it?

Who will benefit?

Who will be the first to notice that things have changed?

Write what you'd like to change in this cloud.

Write your answers in this cloud.

SLEEP STONES

Sleep stones are gentle reminders that sleep is something your body and brain need to get you ready for tomorrow.

Make a set of sleep stones to help you feel ready to sleep. You can keep them in your room and play with them, talk about them with someone, or just look at them at bedtime to help you settle down for sleep.

Think of things that make you feel calm, peaceful, happy, or sleepy to put on the stones. You might choose messages from people who love you, quotes from people you admire, pictures of the moon and stars, patterns you like, your favorite characters, reminders that tomorrow is going to be great, or anything else you find supportive and encouraging.

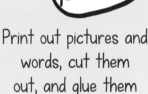

YOU WILL NEED:

- Small or medium stones
- Dishwashing liquid
- Warm water
- Paper towel
- Paint

- Permanent markers
- Printed words
- Scissors
- Glue
- A box

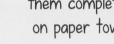

Collect some small or medium-sized stones with at least one fairly flat surface from your garden, or buy them at a nursery or craft shop.

 Wash and dry them completely on paper towel.

 Print out pictures and words, cut them out, and glue them on, or draw and write directly on the stones.

WARNING

Make sure you check with an adult before using any container, and ask them to make sure it's clean and safe for you to use.

Make sure an adult helps you when using scissors and permanent markers.

 You could use a box to keep them in, which you can decorate however you like. Cleaned ice cream containers and empty chocolate boxes are ideal.

PJ DAY

Buddy Bear is having a PJ day, and you are invited!

You could invite some of Buddy's friends along, too!

He is planning to spend the day making things, reading, drawing, napping, watching movies, and doing relaxation exercises.

Can you design his PJs for this restful day?

Fill in the PJs with your own special design, and use all the shapes and colors you want to see him wearing.

Imagine the PJ day you have together, and then draw or write about it.

Try to include lots of interesting details, for example, what you made, what you read, what snacks you had, what movie you watched, where you napped, how you felt, and all the other things you can think of.

TWO STARS
AND A DREAM

It's a good idea to end each day by taking a moment to reflect on what you've enjoyed about your day or what you are grateful for. Try to think of at least two things.

Then, think about something you'd like to happen, achieve, or do tomorrow.

THESE ARE YOUR STARS

THIS IS YOUR DREAM

Choose an adult, family member, or friend to talk to about your two stars and a dream, then record them here with today's date. Keep coming back until you've filled all the stars and dreams.

Can you carry on doing this every evening as part of your routine before bed?

SWEET DREAMS

Want a great way to relax and give your brain and body a rest on a busy day?

Fill in these dream bubbles with special and happy memories you have made in the past with the people or pets you love and who love you.

You can keep some blank and save them for your future memories, or dream up memories you'd like to make happen and add those, too.

Talk to someone at home about these memories as you're relaxing or settling into bed, describing in as much detail as you can how you felt at the time. If you're putting yourself to bed, why not tell your memories to your bedtime bear or cuddly toy?

COLOR THESE IN

Color in these midnight mandalas.

Can you draw your own?

AS YOU DO THIS ACTIVITY, BREATHE DEEPLY AND SLOWLY. KEEP YOUR OUT BREATH A BIT LONGER THAN YOUR IN BREATH BY DOING 3:5 BREATHING.

SORTED!

Everyone has bad dreams from time to time. These happen because your brain works just as hard when you are asleep as it does when you are awake.

It goes over everything it sees, feels, learns, and wonders about during the day and has to decide what to forget, what to remember, how to remember it, and where to put it. It's a bit like when you sort recycling and trash, or organize different piles of laundry.

Sort your thoughts into these baskets, and do some of your brain's work before you go to sleep.

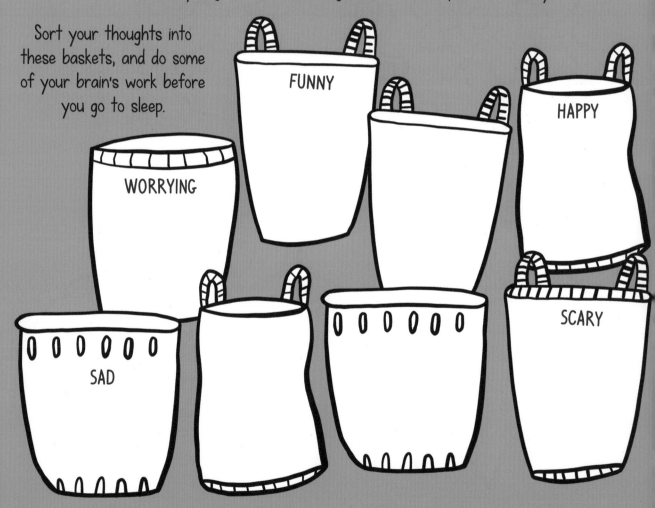

You could also do this activity by writing your thoughts on slips of paper and sorting them into any small baskets or boxes you have at home. You could even draw around the template on the next page to make some boxes if you want to.

DREAM TRAPPER

Bad dreams happen when your brain is making sense of your experiences. It thinks that because you're asleep, you won't notice the work it's doing. It isn't trying to upset or frighten you, and bad dreams don't mean anything.

this is the inside of your trap

Make this dream trapper to catch and overpower your bad dreams, if they happen.

YOU WILL NEED:

- Glue
- Scissors
- Pens

Ask an adult for help when using scissors.

Write or draw anything you remember from the bad dream on a piece of paper, fold it up, close the lid, and trap it in this box until its power has gone.

Then, take it out, rip it up, and pop it in the recycling or compost.

Use the dream trapper again whenever you need to.

MY DREAM TRAPPER

Put your dream trapper anywhere you think it will help you remember not to worry about bad dreams.

INSTRUCTIONS:

• Stick the inside of the trap to cardboard (cereal boxes are perfect for this).

• Color in the words, MY DREAM TRAPPER.

• Decorate the outside of the trapper.*

• Fold it and stick it together, decorated side out, leaving the lid unstuck.

* Write or draw all the things and people that make you feel safe, happy, and brave around the outside and inside of your box.

Add sequins, ribbons, feathers, beads, stickers, or anything you like.

HANDS TOGETHER

Ask an adult for some hand lotion with a great smell that is suitable for you to use.

Smell the lotion together, describing what it reminds you of, saying why you like it, and commenting on anything else you notice about it.

Choose which of you will go first to spend five minutes massaging this lotion all over the other person's hands. Take your time, and gently cover every part. Notice any hurts on their hands, like bitten nails, or grazes.

After five minutes, swap.

Do this activity as often as you like, day or night. Remember, resting and relaxing during the day helps to keep you calm and reduces worry and stress.

PILLOW
TALK

Lying in bed can feel cozy and lovely when you are relaxed and comfortable. If that's not how you always feel at bedtime, it's probably because you still have things you need to say, or things you want to hear.

Write on this pillowcase all the things you like talking about before you go to sleep. It might be going over the day you've had, planning your breakfast, discussing the solar system, inventing a time machine, or anything that matters to you.

Fill this pillowcase with all the things you like to hear at bedtime.

Choose things that make your mind feel calm and your body feel soft, like, *it's going to be OK*, *you are so loved*, *you did well today*.

Show this page to an adult, or make your own posters of the pillowcases and put them up as a reminder by your bed. If you like, you could say these things to your teddy bear or cuddly toy.

PILLOW PALS

We all need a special pal who is full of cuddles, listens carefully, and is ready to help us get comfy night after night.

This Pillow Pal is easy to make and will brighten up your day – and night!

YOU WILL NEED:

- A clean, plain pillowcase and pillow
- Fabric markers

OPTIONAL:

- Scraps of fabric
- Scissors
- Needle and thread

Ask an adult for help when using scissors or sewing needles.

Ask an adult to help you choose a pillowcase and pillow, and always ask for help if you are cutting and sewing.

Make sure you don't leave a sharp needle somewhere where it could hurt you.

INSTRUCTIONS:

Lay your empty pillowcase on a table or flat surface.

Decide what you'd like your Pillow Pal to be – maybe a rabbit, mouse, puppy, or kitten?

It's up to you!

Put a newspaper or other protective layer such as a wipe-clean cloth inside the pillowcase to prevent the pens from marking the other side of the fabric or the surface underneath.

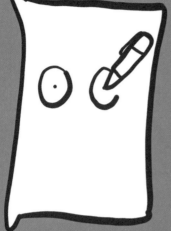

Draw on the eyes, nose, and mouth with your fabric markers.

If you want to, you can add ears, whiskers, or a tail by drawing them on, or use scraps of fabric that you cut out and sew on.

Pop the pillow in, and say hello to your new Pillow Pal!

MOONWALK

Ever been for a walk in your PJs?

It's great fun to do.

Ask an adult to take you for a walk once the light outside is fading.

Being outside in dim light causes your brain to notice it's nearly nighttime.

It responds, and understands that you should be preparing for sleep, creating the chemical melatonin to have you yawning in no time.

It can help to reset your body clock if it's gone a bit wonky because of screens, worry, stress, or being too busy.

Take a flashlight with you if you want to.

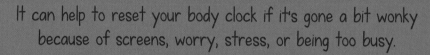

Your body clock is managed by a part of your brain called the hypothalamus. It makes sure you know when to sleep, wake up, eat and drink, as well as keeping you at the right temperature.

As you walk, really listen to the different sounds you can hear.

Look at the tops of trees or buildings and see which stars are already shining.

Notice where the moon is in the sky and what shape it is.

You can also do this activity in your yard, if you have one, or it's something you can try if you go camping.

Make sure you're warm enough and you have proper shoes on your feet.

A ROOM OF ONE'S OWN

If your bedroom feels calm and relaxing, it will be good for getting to sleep. Look around your room and decide how you can make it the best it can be to help you SLEEP TIGHT!

THINGS TO CONSIDER

Think about how your toys and other items are stored – can they be tidied easily? Can you make it dark enough to sleep comfortably?

Do you have something cuddly to take to bed? Do you have precious photos around you for comfort? Are your screens tucked away safely so you can relax?

It's not always possible to make changes to your room, but you can always design your own dream bedroom. On a separate sheet of paper, or in a sketchpad, draw your ideal bedroom and make sure to include all the things you'd include if you could have your room exactly how you'd like it.

SOME IDEAS TO HELP YOU:

- A bed
- Cozy covers
- A chair
- A desk
- Curtains or blinds
- A light
- Photos and posters
- Trinkets and souvenirs

Why not make a 3-D version of your ideal room using an old cardboard box and furniture made from cereal boxes, fabric, and other clean recycled items?

DEVICE DORMITORY

We know that using screens and devices in the hours before bed is not a good idea. The games or activities you use them for get your brain pinging and whirring, while the light from the device itself disrupts your brain's ability to switch off and sleep.

Devices need to switch off, too! Shall we give them somewhere cozy, cool, and comfy to spend their nights?

Design and make a device dormitory for your favorite screens to help get a good night's sleep – for you and them!

Your device dormitory can look exactly how you want it to.

MATERIALS

- You could use old cardboard or plastic boxes, milk containers, cereal boxes, or whatever recyclable items you have, to make it.

- You might like to use scraps of fabric or an old piece of clothing for bedding or curtains – or you could knit or crochet items!

- You'll find scissors, glue, sticky tape, and pens useful.

- It can be helpful to start by making a list of the materials you think you'll need – or just work it out as you go along, if that's more your style.

DRAW YOUR DESIGN HERE:

HELPFUL HINT
Don't forget to measure your devices
first to be sure they will fit! Ask an
adult to help you with any cutting.

DUVET DESIGN

What things do you find the most comforting?

Maybe you relax most when you think about people in your family,
your pets, your friends, your team, your best book, your
favorite meal, a great memory, or something else?

Imagine having your own duvet cover to hold these
things close to you as you sleep soundly through the night.

Elsie and Eddie have designed comforting duvet covers with
their favorite things for you to color in.

Design your very own duvet cover. Add as much detail as you like.

You can make a matching pillowcase, or leave it plain if you prefer.

Don't forget to put your bedtime bear or cuddly toy on the bed somewhere, too.

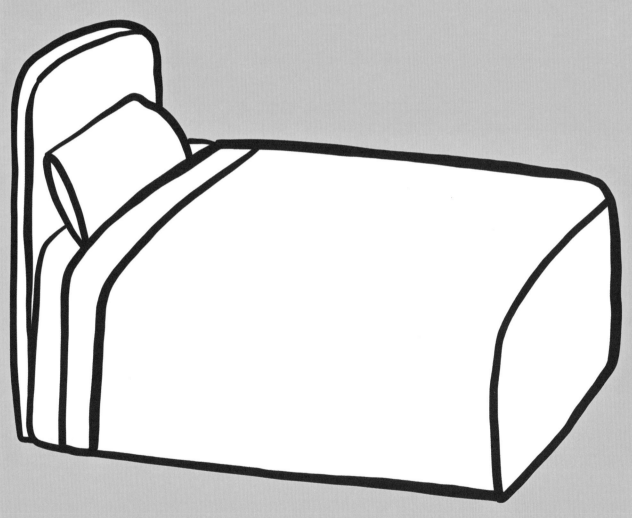

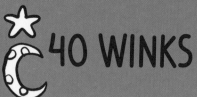

40 WINKS

Not yet ready for bed? This activity will help you wind down and let your brain know it's almost, but not quite, time for snoozing.

Sit or lie down somewhere comfortable – the ideal place to do this is in bed, naturally! Have a low light on if possible, or you can do this just as well in the dark.

Start 3:5 breathing and make sure your eyes are wide-open.
Don't close them! Whatever happens, keep them open.
You don't want to accidentally fall asleep while you're still doing the activity.

After a few minutes of 3:5 breathing, close your eyes and say "one" out loud or in your head.

Only close your eyes for the shortest amount of time possible, then open them wide again.

Next, do the same thing and say "two," but keep your eyes closed for a tiny bit longer this time – as tiny as you can manage.

Keep going like this for each number up to 30, making your eyes stay shut for a tiny bit longer each time.

At 31, try to picture yourself floating on a friendly cloud among the bright, shiny stars, and keep your eyes closed so you can enjoy it. Imagine looking down on your street and watching everyone getting into bed for a good night's sleep.

Open your eyes when you feel like it.

Keep going until you get to 39. At 40, you can keep your eyes closed if you want to, or open them – YOUR CHOICE.

CATCH YOUR BREATH

Don't wait until nighttime to catch up on some of that delicious, refreshing, rest and relaxation!

Sometimes life can be really busy and your mind and body have to work extra hard to keep up.

We know that Bob can become overwhelmed and tired if there's too much going on, so that by bedtime, he struggles to switch off and fall asleep.

GOING FOR A WALK

READING A BOOK OR COMIC

MEDITATION

YOGA

DRAWING

3:5 BREATHING

WRITING

LOOKING AT NATURE

Give Bob a break and catch your breath during the day in whatever ways you enjoy most. The activities in this book might give you some other ideas, too.

Fill the leaves on the tree with all the different ways you can unwind and relax.

TWINKLE, TWINKLE, LITTLE STAR

Ever wanted to be able to draw your own stars? Follow the instructions and see how easy it is to draw fantastic stars whenever you like.

Once you've gotten the hang of it, try to draw them without taking your pen off the page. Then fill a piece of paper with as many stars as you want and color them in!

 **1** Draw two sides of a mountain, starting at the bottom of the left side.

 2 Draw a diagonal line from the bottom of the mountain and out to the side.

 **3** Draw a horizontal line across the mountain to the same distance on the other side.

 4 Draw another diagonal line to the bottom of the other side of the mountain.

 **5** Color in your star so it shines brightly! Why not draw a whole galaxy of stars?

STARGAZING

Look into the night sky and try to find as many stars as you can. Turn off the lights so you can see them twinkling.

If it's cloudy, or there are lots of lights outside, it might be harder to spot the stars, but then you can watch the clouds flying through the sky instead.

Spend as long as you want doing this. It works even better if you can do this outside, but if you can't, through a closed window is just as good.

YOU COULD TRY TO LEARN THE NAMES OF THE DIFFERENT STARS AND THE SHAPES THEY MAKE USING AN APP OR REFERENCE BOOK.

Color in these twinkly stars. As you finish each one, write something you are grateful for, happy about, or looking forward to inside or underneath it. You might want to include people, places, pets, events, or absolutely anything that matters to you.

Even when you've filled in all the stars, you can draw your own in the empty spaces or on a blank piece of paper.

TALK 12

Bob needs regular rest during the day to help him SLEEP TIGHT! at night.

Some days are so busy! If you find that you are always on the go, and you don't usually take time to slow down, this is a great way to rest and relax.

Grab a timer and someone to talk to, then start talking!
If you're alone, talk to a pet or your favorite cuddly toy.

Talk for 12 minutes about anything you like.

Make a list of all the things you love to chatter about so you can come back to it and get ideas when you need them.

You could choose topics such as memories, funny stories, books, hobbies, sports, fashion, animals – whatever you can talk nonstop about for 12 minutes or longer! GO!

Fill in this grid every time you unwind with TALK 12!

WRITE WHAT YOU TALKED ABOUT	WRITE HOW LONG YOU TALKED FOR	WRITE WHO YOU TALKED TO

NO MONSTERS ALLOWED

Ever since humans have existed, children all over the world have worried about monsters at bedtime.

There are no real monsters. You can SLEEP TIGHT!

Color these imaginary, scary monsters. Draw some of your own, too. Remember, they are not real, they are from your imagination.

Trap your monsters in jars without air, food, or drink. They could have a jar each or all go in one together.

Label the jars with their names if you want to.

Put the jars where you can see them every day. Trapped in the jar, they can't grow or scare you. You're in charge of them.

When they no longer bother you, just rip them up into tiny pieces and throw them in the recycling, or compost them and recycle the jars.

I AM GOOD ENOUGH

SLEEPOVER

Who would you invite to a sleepover?

You can choose anyone you want to invite, perhaps from books, history, your family, or friends.

WRITE AN INVITATION HERE.

Remember to say what exciting things are going to happen, and if you need them to do anything or bring anything to the sleepover.

IMAGINE YOURSELF HAVING THE SLEEPOVER. DRAW OR WRITE ABOUT IT HERE.

MAKEOVER

Buddy Bear wants to try out some new looks for a sleepover. Use your creativity to help him try out different looks so he stands out from the sleuth.

A group of bears is called a sleuth.

SLEEP DETECTIVE

Are you a supersleuth?

Sleuth also means detective!

What stops you from getting to sleep or going back to sleep?
Are you too hot? Is it too light? Do you feel too worried?

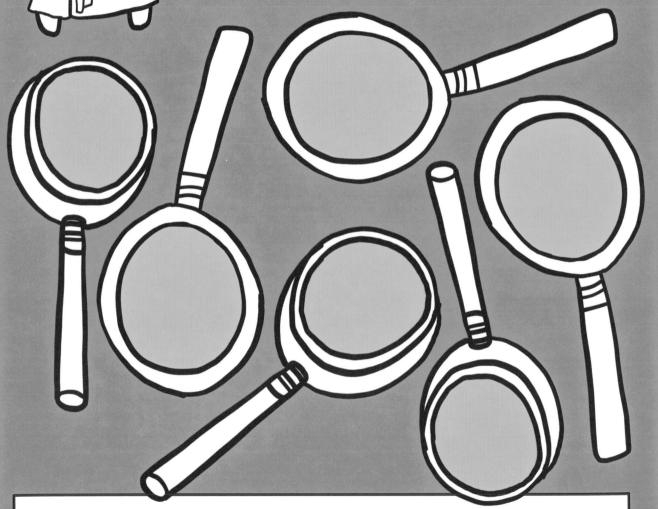

Every time you work out what is getting in your way, add it here.

Talk to an adult to help you if you want. Look through the book and find the activities that are the most helpful for you to conquer these problems. You can do it!

A BIT OF SHUT-EYE

Find a quiet place to do this activity.

You can do the activity any time of the day or night to rest your eyes, mind, and body.

Getting rest and relaxation during the day is an important way to help you stay healthy and SLEEP TIGHT! at night.

Bob will thank you for slowing down regularly and unwinding.

Pay attention to your breathing and slow it down. Do 3:5 breathing if you like.

Look at the ceiling or sky with your eyes wide-open for around ten seconds.

REMEMBER not to look directly at the sun at any time. It's always safe to look at the moon.

Close your eyes and squeeze your eye muscles firmly for around ten seconds. Don't use your hands to press on or rub your eyes. Then relax your eye muscles, but keep them closed.

Watch as the patterns, shapes, squiggles, colors, and dots move and fade away.

Try experimenting with this activity, and vary the amount of time your eyes are closed to see what difference it makes to what you see.

Draw what you saw, if you want to.

THREE THINGS

Once you're tucked up in bed, here's an activity you can do to help you settle down for a wonderful sleep. It's also really helpful to do this activity in the daytime whenever you need to relax and take some time for yourself.

Breathe in for a count of 3, slowly and deeply into your tummy, and breathe out for a count of 5, just as slowly. This is one set of 3:5.

Close your eyes and start 3:5 breathing.

After about ten sets of 3:5, open your eyes and notice three things you can see, one at a time.

Close your eyes again.

Notice three things you can hear, one at a time. These things may be in your room, outside your room, or outside where you live.

Next, notice three things you can feel with your body, one at a time. You might be able to feel the pillow under your head, the warmth from your bedding, or your own heart beating.

Now imagine three things you'd love to see – these can be totally random or connected to each other, whatever you prefer. You might imagine a unicorn galloping across the fields, an incredible shot taken by your favorite sports player, or a book character waving at you.

When that's all done, imagine three sounds you'd love to hear – maybe the cheer of a crowd when you do something amazing, people singing "Happy Birthday" to you, or the laughter of your friends.

Finally, imagine three things you'd love to feel – perhaps the splash of water on a warm beach, the sand under your feet on the surface of the moon, or a comforting hug from someone you love. Let your mind linger on these feelings, and take as much time as you like to really enjoy them. SLEEP TIGHT!

TOMORROW IS ANOTHER DAY

COLOR THIS IN

Ask an adult to describe to you how you look when you are sleeping, then draw and color a picture of yourself sleeping soundly and having a wonderful, happy, funny, or silly dream.

PICTURE THIS

Fill the dream cloud with things from your dream.

You could draw a scene from it or make a storyboard of different scenes.

You can write about your dream if you prefer.

CHANGING FACES, CHANGING PLACES

Have you ever noticed how dreams can go all over the place? How they can jump from the beach to the stars, into the park, and then back to school?

People change into each other and can do and say some things that seem very strange when you think about them afterward.

Let's turn this into a fun game for the whole household to play before bedtime! Having a good laugh with people you love is great preparation for bedtime. Laughing is the perfect way to rest and relax at any time to help you slow down and feel calm.

You might also be able to come up with your own version of this game and try out lots of different ideas.

INSTRUCTIONS:

Give a piece of paper to each person playing.

Players turn their papers to portrait (shortest side at the top and bottom) and fold them into four sections, by folding them in half from the bottom and then in half again.

Then, unfold the paper and number the sections going down, 1 to 4.

Refold so that only the top section (section 1) can be seen.

YOU'RE READY TO START!

It might be helpful to set a time limit for drawing on each section.

NO PEEKING UNTIL THE PICTURES ARE FINISHED!

CHANGING FACES

1 Players draw a head, neck, and face, with hair, in the top section of their papers (1) – they can choose exactly how it looks. Make sure the bottom of the neck goes into section 2 slightly. Now fold the paper so no one can see it and so section 2 is on top, right way up. No looking at what has been drawn until the game is finished! Players pass this to another player.

2 Players draw the top of a body from the front, side, or back, in section 2 – only the top of it, though! It could be a human, a robot, an animal, an insect, or whatever! Make sure the picture comes all the way to the bottom of the section and very slightly into section 3. Fold the paper so no one can see it and so section 3 is on top, right way up. Players pass this to another player.

3 Players draw the bottom half of a body in section 3, using the same idea as before or something completely different. Make sure the picture comes all the way to the bottom of the section of the paper. Fold the paper so no one can see it and so section 4 is on top, right way up. Players pass this to another player.

4 Players draw legs and feet in section 4 – tall, short, knobbly, furry, one, two, four hundred! It's up to them. Players pass to another player.

5 Players open up the drawings and show each other the finished pictures!

THE OTHER SIDE

Although you can only see and feel it in the daytime, the sun is always shining.

It never stops. It's always up there in the sky bringing
light and warmth to people all over the world.

When you look up at the bright moon in the dark, night sky, the light you
see is reflected from the sun by the moon's surface. Even when it's taking
daytime to different countries on the other side of the world, we know
that the sun will come back around to bring us daytime all over again.

Draw a picture of someone on the other side of the world enjoying
daytime while you're getting ready to sleep through the night. Think about
who they are, what they enjoy, and what they might be doing until it gets
dark where they are – until the sun comes back around to you.

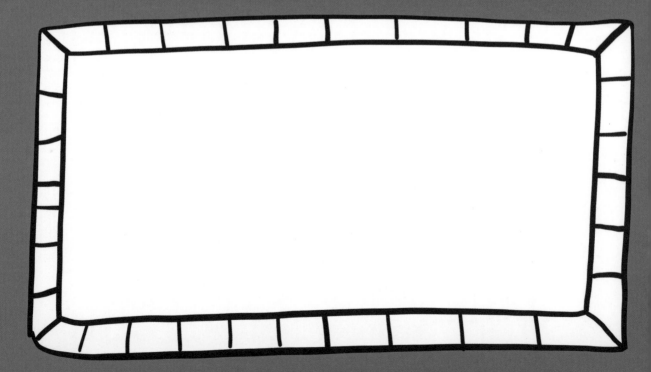

Day always follows night. The moon is our promise that a new day is on the way.

Friendship, love, happiness, and laughter are like the sun because they are always there, even when you can't see them or feel them. They might be reflected in your memories or thoughts until they come back around.

Make a list of all the people and things that are still there in your life, even when you can't see them. Remember, they will come back around to you in time.

WANING CRESCENT

FULL MOON

WAXING CRESCENT

LAND OF NOD

Color this dreamscape and add whatever you want to it. Anything goes – it's a dream! Be as creative as you like.

I FEEL THE NEED

Bedtime can often bring out feelings that need to be heard. Sometimes you can go all day without a care, and then suddenly you have all kinds of needs that bubble up as bedtime gets closer.

Working out what you need to help you feel calm and ready to **SLEEP TIGHT!** is a great idea for you because it makes you feel more in control, and it's great for your adults too because they can help you in the right way.

Make yourself a set of I NEED cards to help your bedtimes feel positive and happy. Remember to add this activity to your bedtime routine so you have time for it. Show the cards to an adult to explain what you need. Encourage others in your family to make their own set of I NEED cards, too.

YOU WILL NEED:

- Blank cards; you could use:

  - paper

  - sticky notes

  – blank playing cards

  – cutout shapes from old greeting cards or packaging

- A list of your needs – as many as you want to cover all the feelings you can think of.

Every time you notice a new feeling, make a card for it and add it to your set.

I'M WORRIED, I NEED

_____reassurance_____

I'M UPSET, I NEED

_____a hug_____

I'M HAPPY, I NEED

_____

I'M BORED, I NEED

_____

I'M _____,

I NEED

_____

I'M _____,

I NEED

_____

I'M CROSS, I NEED

_____some time alone_____

I'M _____,

I NEED

_____

I'M _____,

I NEED

_____

SHARE BEAR

Sharing is caring!

Sometimes, you might feel like you want to share something that's playing on your mind with your adults.

Maybe you want to tell them something exciting that happened, or is going to happen, something that's bothering you, or something about how you're feeling.

You might want to give them a compliment, or ask for their opinion or advice about a particular problem.

Why not turn one of your teddy bears into a Share Bear?

Write down what's on your mind on a piece of paper, add the date, and leave enough room for a reply. Pop your note into the envelope, which you can then place on the tummy of a teddy bear or other cuddly toy somewhere your adults will know to look for it. They can write you a reply and pop it back where you will know to look for it in the morning.

INSTRUCTIONS:

Cut out the template, fold along the dotted lines, and stick the bottom and sides together to make the envelope.

(Always ask an adult for help when using scissors.)

You could make a second envelope to keep all your old notes in once you receive replies.

If you plan to make another envelope, be sure to trace around the cutout template on another piece of paper or cardboard before you put your envelope together.

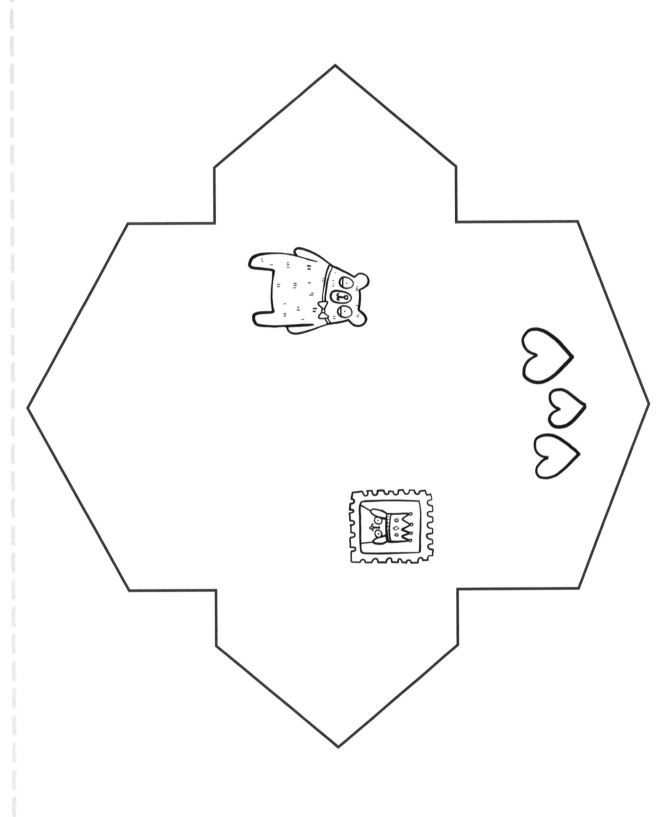

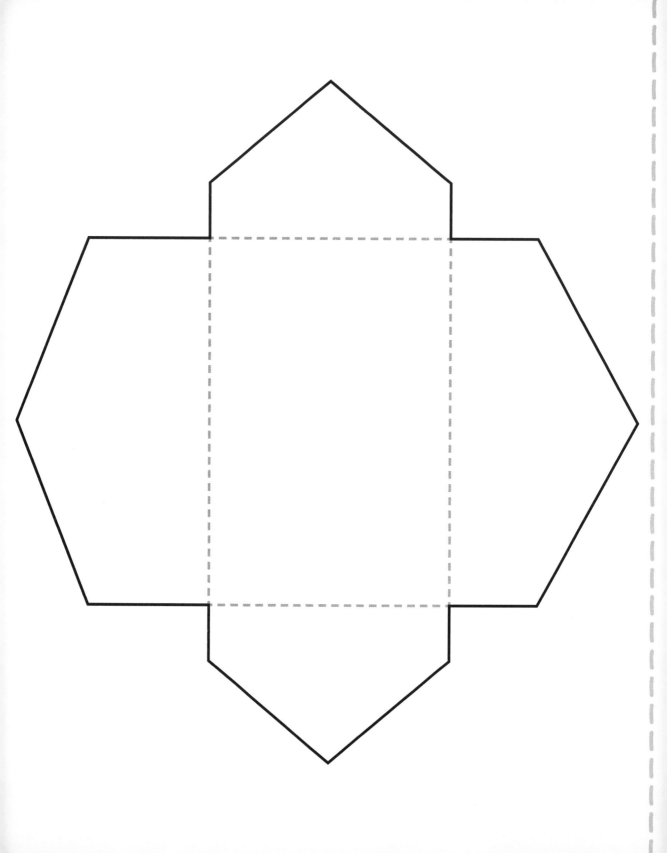

BOB TOKENS

Fill in these tokens to use at bedtime when something isn't feeling right. You can pick a token that will comfort you, and show it to your adults.

This will help Bob to feel listened to and will settle him down so you can snooze all night.

Make your tokens and store them in a box. You could decorate the box with stickers, pictures, or wrapping paper.

If you need more tokens, you can make your own, or write on the back of these.

Talk to your adults to agree on how many tokens you can use each night when you need them.

AN ACTIVITY FROM SLEEP TIGHT! 			A CUDDLE 
	A DRINK OF WATER 		
A STORY 		A CHAT 	

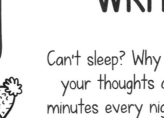

Getting your thoughts out helps Bob calm down and lets the melatonin flow.

WRITE NIGHT

Can't sleep? Why not try drawing or writing your thoughts and worries down for 20 minutes every night when you get into bed?

You could choose a special notebook to write in. Use a dim light if you can, not a bright light. You can share your notebook with your adults if you want to, or keep it somewhere private.

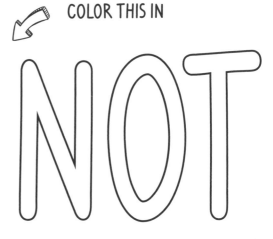 COLOR THIS IN

I AM NOT ALONE

MINDFUL MUSCLES

Gradually relaxing your body and muscles will help you to get to sleep more quickly.

Try this activity to quiet Bob down for a daytime rest or at bedtime to make you feel ready for sleep.

Lie down and get comfortable.

It would be helpful if an adult is able to read the instructions aloud.

Put your arms by your sides and your legs out straight.

Start 3:5 breathing.

Breathe in for 3 slowly and deeply into your tummy, and breathe out for 5 just as slowly.

Tighten up your face by scrunching your cheeks up to your eyes. Clench your teeth.

Hold this as you breathe in for a count of 3.

Breathe out slowly for a count of 5, and gently let your face muscles relax.

Repeat this once or twice.

Next, tighten up your neck, and pull your shoulders up to your ears.

Hold this as you breathe in for a count of 3.

Breathe out slowly for a count of 5, and gently let your neck and shoulder muscles relax back.

Repeat this once or twice.

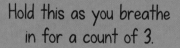

Next, tighten up your arms and hands by gently rolling your fists up under your chin.

Hold this as you breathe in for a count of 3.

Breathe out slowly for a count of 5, and gently let your arm and hand muscles relax by your sides.

Repeat this once or twice.

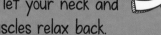

Next, tighten up your chest by pulling your shoulders in front of you.

Hold this as you breathe in for a count of 3.

Breathe out slowly for a count of 5, and gently let your chest muscles and shoulders relax back.

Repeat this once or twice.

Next, tense up your legs by pointing your toes to the stars.

Hold this as you breathe in for a count of 3.

Breathe out slowly for a count of 5, and gently let your leg muscles relax as you drop your toes.

Repeat this once or twice.

Next, scrunch up your feet by curling your toes toward your heels.

Hold this as you breathe in for a count of 3.

Breathe out slowly for a count of 5, and gently let your foot muscles relax.

Repeat this once or twice.

Next, tighten up your tummy by sucking it in.

Hold this as you breathe in for a count of 3.

Breathe out slowly for a count of 5, and gently let your tummy muscles relax.

Repeat this once or twice.

Next, tighten up your buttocks by clenching them.

Hold this as you breathe in for a count of 3.

Breathe out slowly for a count of 5, and gently let your buttock muscles relax back.

Repeat this once or twice.

Spend some time enjoying how relaxed you feel.

If you'd like to, you can repeat the whole process, working back up your body to your face.

Now, you can SLEEP TIGHT!

PACK UP YOUR TROUBLES

Make a **SLEEP TIGHT!** kit full of things that will help to relax you, encourage melatonin, and help you get back to sleep if you wake in the night.

Bob loves a **SLEEP TIGHT!** kit.

INSTRUCTIONS:

Choose a pillowcase that you love for your kit.

Decide what is going into your kit – look for things that make you feel safe, brave, and happy, and that you can enjoy without putting the lights on, if possible.

You can decorate your pillowcase or leave it plain, whatever you prefer.

Add a short ribbon or an elastic band to keep everything inside until you want to take it out.

You can change your kit contents as often as you want.

Here are some things you could put in your **SLEEP TIGHT!** kit.

CUDDLY TOY

POM-POM

BLANKET

HEAD BAND

SPECIAL PHOTO

SLEEP STONES

HAND LOTION

POSTCARD

LETTER

BUBBLE WRAP

FRIENDSHIP BRACELET

Write your ideas for things to put in your **SLEEP TIGHT!** kit.

You could show your list to an adult to make sure each item is safe for you to use when you're in bed.

SMELLY BEAR

Ask an adult for some scent that you like the smell of, or that reminds you of feeling safe and happy. Make sure you don't use anything you're allergic to.

Put a small dab onto your bedtime bear or cuddly toy, and let the familiar smell help you to drop off to sleep.

Sometimes, asking to borrow your adult's pillow is a good way to get the same result without using a scent. Make sure you give them your pillow as a swap!

WRITE OR DRAW ON THIS PILLOW ALL THE SMELLS YOU FIND COMFORTING OR FAMILIAR.

Lavender is a scent that helps Bob settle down – he LOVES it!

BEAR HUGS

Bears give fantastic hugs! Why not ask for a bear hug from someone you love right now? It feels so good in your tummy.

DRAW OR WRITE HOW IT FEELS IN THIS BEAR'S TUMMY.

Be careful when you hug pets - they don't like it too tight!

Don't forget, your bedtime bear or cuddly toy is always happy to get a bear hug from you, day or night!

DREAM TICKET

Where would you like to go to in your dreams?

Who with?

What will you do when you get there?

Think about somewhere you'd love to go –
it can be a real place or an imaginary place.

It can be from a book, a film, or
a memory – or anywhere you like!

Make yourself a ticket, get into your bed, and
close your eyes. There's nothing stopping you!

You can make as many tickets
as you like using blank paper
once you've filled this one in.

I WOULD LIKE TO GO TO: _____

_____

I WOULD LIKE TO GO WITH: _____

_____

WHEN WE GET THERE, WE WILL: _____

_____

RISE AND SHINE

Before you snuggle down for the night, fill these brilliant suns with all the fun things you are looking forward to doing tomorrow after a fantastic night's sleep!

Write today's date under each sun.

Keep coming back until they're all filled in.

Don't forget that you can make your own suns on blank paper when these are finished.

WORRY TIME

Ask an adult at home to do this activity with you.

If there's more than one adult, they could take turns if you like. It works well at any time of the day or evening and can help you to relax throughout the day to make sure Bob doesn't get too worked up.

Agree on a time to do this regularly for 10 minutes every day, or every evening, or just when you need it.

During these 10 minutes, speak about your worries and fears and nothing else. Your adult will just listen lovingly and won't try to fix anything in this time (they can help you with it later). If you run out of worries, just sit together until the time is up.

After 10 minutes do 10 slow, deep breaths together, holding hands, and look directly into each other's eyes.

Then have a 10-second hug.

Why not make a worry jar? If you find worries coming up at other times, just write them on scraps of paper, pop them in the jar, and take them out at WORRY TIME. Chuck them in the recycling or compost when you've dealt with them.

HERE ARE SOME GOOD WAYS FOR ADULTS TO LISTEN LOVINGLY — CIRCLE THE ONES YOU'D LIKE YOUR ADULT TO SAY.

I'm listening

It's OK to be afraid

I want to be here for you

I'm here with you

I can see why that is scary for you

This feeling will pass

I will help you work it out

It's really hard for you

It doesn't feel fair

I hear you

I'll stay close so we can sort that out together when you're ready

Tell me more about it

I can support you to SLEEP TIGHT!

You've got what it takes

HAPPY TIME

YOU WILL NEED:

- A clean, dry jar with a lid
- Scraps of paper or sticky notes
- Paper for making a label
- Glue to stick the label onto the jar

Every time you do something fun, happy, brave, exciting, or lovely, write it down on a scrap of paper and pop it into your HAPPY TIME jar!

Spend a few minutes after WORRY TIME going through your HAPPY TIME jar and talk about the times you've looked at.

HAPPY TIME will help you to SLEEP TIGHT!

YOGA

Buddy and Bob know that yoga and other exercises help to relax your body and prepare you for a good night's sleep. Hold each of these poses for as long as feels comfortable before moving into the next pose. Try to do the yoga poses an hour or two before you go to bed and you'll **SLEEP TIGHT!**

CRESCENT MOON POSE

Stand tall, with arms by your sides, toes touching, and your feet slightly apart. Breathe in and lift your arms, pressing your palms together above your head. Bend to one side and keep breathing gently. Come back to your starting position.

Repeat, but bend to the other side.

Come back to your starting position.

Say out loud: **I AM RELAXED.**

LOTUS POSE

Sit down and stretch your legs out in front of your body. Bend one leg at a time and place your foot on top of the opposite thigh. Let your knee touch the ground comfortably. Repeat with your other leg. Press your palms together in front of your heart and sit tall with relaxed shoulders. Close your eyes and breathe slowly. Relax your whole body.

If it is more comfortable, press the soles of your feet together rather than putting your feet on your thighs.

Say out loud: **I AM BRAVE.**

STAR POSE

Stand tall and open your legs as far apart as you can. Turn your toes forward and stand with your weight on both feet. Stretch your back up tall, and your arms and fingers out wide with your palms facing the floor.

Relax your shoulders. Breathe deeply and send light and energy to your toes and fingers. Imagine yourself shining brightly above the world.

Say out loud: I AM LIGHT.

HAPPY BABY POSE

Lie on your back. Breathe out as you bend your knees into your tummy. Keep breathing gently. Hold the outsides of your feet with your hands. Open your knees a little bit wider than your body and bring them up to your armpits. Keep your ankles directly above your knees.

Say out loud: I AM SAFE.

SLEEP POSE (ALSO CALLED CHILD'S POSE)

Kneel with your knees wide apart. Gently sit on your heels. Breathe in and sit up straight, stretching your back upward. Breathe out and lower your upper body so your heart and chest rest on your thighs. Keep breathing smoothly. Place your forehead on the floor. Stretch your arms back along your sides, on the ground, with your palms facing up.

Say out loud: I AM HAPPY.

SLEEPYHEAD

Take a deep breath, stretch your arms out, and YAWN! Imagine you are a great big bear and yawn as loudly and for as long as you can.

Get everyone else involved, too!

Did you know that if someone else yawns, it's very likely you will too? And if YOU yawn, they will too!

Test it out with your family and friends.

Make a list of who you can make yawn just by yawning in front of them.

SLEEP CYCLES

When we sleep, we move through cycles of being in light sleep, deep sleep, and dream sleep. These cycles repeat every ninety minutes or so. Everyone wakes up a few times in the night during the sleep cycle, even if they don't remember it.

You can fall back to sleep easily if you are relaxed and feeling safe, brave, and happy.

Use the activities in this book to help YOU feel relaxed, safe, brave, and happy.

Make sure you do this activity in the morning, not when you wake up in the night!

Fill in one section of these bicycle wheels every time you manage to sleep all night or get back to sleep after waking up in the night!

NIGHTY NIGHT

When the nighttime gets on top of you,
there's a helpful thing that you can do.

Something simple can make it better:
pick up and read a heartfelt letter!

Choose some special paper and write yourself a letter,
remembering to include supportive messages for
yourself and a reminder of the ways that you have
discovered that work to help you get to sleep quickly.

Sometimes it helps to
hear why you are loved
and how important
you are. Ask someone
you live with, a family
member, or a friend to
write you a letter that
you can read any time
you're struggling to fall
asleep or to get back
to sleep. Tell them that
this letter will be used
to help you to relax, feel
comfortable, and settle
down to sleep.

Add any pictures
you want to
your letter.

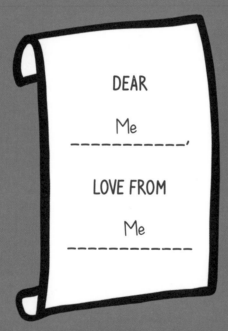

DEAR

Me
_____,

LOVE FROM

Me
_____

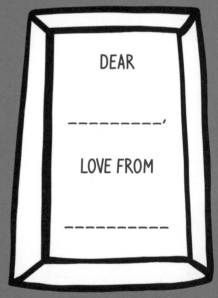

DEAR

_____,

LOVE FROM

_____

Whenever you need to,
just pick up your letters
and remember how
special and unique you
are. You could keep them
in your SLEEP TIGHT! kit,
if you like.

UP THE WOODEN HILL

Ready to create the perfect bedtime routine for yourself? Let's do it!

You are about to SLEEP TIGHT! tonight and every night. Ask an adult to work through this activity with you.

INSTRUCTIONS:

⭐ 1 Turn the page and draw your face on the flag to show how you feel now that you can SLEEP TIGHT!

⭐ 2 Cut out the poster on the next page and put it up in your room or in the kitchen.

⭐ 3 Cut out the bedtime task symbol shapes (on the next page).

⭐ 4 Create and perfect your bedtime routine.

Choose which bedtime tasks you'll do first, and put these on the bottom step. Then do the same for all the other steps, one at a time, until you reach the top.

Find a very special activity that you love to go on the top step to launch you into sleep.

Try out different routines by moving the tasks around using sticky tack, and keep changing the order until it's just right for you and your family.

Cut out these bedtime-task shapes. Go back to Buddy Bear's duvet at the start of the book, and fill in the blank shapes with your favorite activities to include them in your routine.

You can also use the blanks to design your own bedtime tasks.

THE BIT FOR GROWN-UPS

This activity book is perfect for parents and caregivers, teachers, learning mentors, social workers, coaches, therapists, and youth leaders who want to help young people develop healthy sleep patterns.

We all need regular, reliable, and refreshing sleep in order to function well during the day and to be in the right frame of mind for learning and concentrating. However, lots of children experience difficulty with sleeping which often means a tired family who feel emotional, irritable, and increasingly anxious. Bedtime can become a very tricky experience that feels like a battle of wills.

Children are very resilient and, in a loving and nurturing environment, will often work through problems and difficult times without needing additional help. If sleep problems develop into more than a passing phase, it's time to tackle them before poor sleep becomes a habit. They need to feel relaxed, safe, brave, and happy if they are to drop off to sleep easily and stay asleep through the night. SLEEP TIGHT! offers the chance for your child to explore, express, and explain their difficulties and open up the conversation with you. The fun activities build resilience, improve relaxation and general well-being, increase inner calm and courage, inspire understanding of what's keeping them awake, empower them, and encourage a positive sense of their ability to SLEEP TIGHT! They'll learn the benefits of a great bedtime routine, which you can help them create to suit your family's needs and prepare them for sleep.

Your child can use SLEEP TIGHT! independently, but they may want to share some of the pages with you. They may also need you to read out instructions for some of the bedtime relaxation activities.

If your child has **ADHD, autism,** or **anxiety,** their sleep is likely to prove more difficult at times. A weighted blanket might help them to feel safer and more secure. They may need to learn specific relaxation and self-soothing techniques, and establish a predictable routine and structure, which this book will support you in helping them to achieve. In time, they will be able to settle independently, with patience and regular referral back to the techniques. It's a good idea to tackle the causes of anxiety if possible – there are many other books in this series to support you with that.

HOW TO HELP YOUR CHILD WITH SLEEP PROBLEMS

In order to release melatonin to encourage tiredness and sleep, your child's brain has to notice that it's getting toward bedtime. Using screens disrupts this process, so it's a good idea to switch off two hours before bed. In the summer months, the lighter evenings may add to sleep problems, so keep rooms dim if possible. A warm (not hot) bath or shower before bed is beneficial because it's relaxing and causes a small drop in body temperature, which is essential for falling asleep. Like adults, all children are different. If you are consistently battling with bedtimes, it's worth considering whether it's the right bedtime for your child, or whether a small shift could eliminate some of the problems. Children need between 10 and 11 hours of sleep a night at this age.

Nightmares and bad dreams are a normal part of childhood. Remind your child that they are just the result of a hardworking brain that's trying to make sense of the world. They don't have any meaning and are not real. Comfort and reassurance that they are safe and brave are good strategies to use to get them back to sleep. **Night terrors** happen when your child moves between phases of sleep and are particularly distressing for adults to see. Children don't usually remember them, and the best thing to do is to wait for it to pass and then take them gently back to bed.

Poor sleep has been linked to **weight gain,** so it's important to encourage a healthy lifestyle which includes regular exercise and drinking plenty of water. It's best not to have a large meal or do vigorous exercise within two hours of bedtime. A snack with a balance of carbohydrates, fats, and protein can help children to feel ready to sleep if offered around an hour before bedtime.

Bed-wetting can cause disruption, further tiredness, and frustration. Seek expert support through your doctor or school nurse if this becomes a problem.

Where you feel that everything has been tried, remember that there are sleep experts and therapists you can contact to help you further. Look for support from registered professionals. If your child's sleep problems persist or escalate rather than decrease, you can talk to the doctor, school nurse, or one of the organizations listed below.

KIDSHEALTH

Physician-reviewed information and advice on children's health and parenting issues for parents, kids, teens, and educators.

www.kidshealth.org

CHILD MIND INSTITUTE

Insights and advice on facing the challenges that many families share. Available in English and Spanish.

Search "sleep" on the Topics A-Z page for helpful articles.

childmind.org